Gratitude

MADE SIMPLE

A daily journal for
appreciating life's gifts

PETER PAUPER PRESS, INC.
WHITE PLAINS, NEW YORK

PETER PAUPER PRESS
Fine Books and Gifts Since 1928

OUR COMPANY

In 1928, at the age of twenty-two, Peter Beilenson began printing books on a small press in the basement of his parents' home in Larchmont, New York. Peter—and later, his wife, Edna—sought to create fine books that sold at "prices even a pauper could afford."

Today, still family owned and operated, Peter Pauper Press continues to honor our founders' legacy—and our customers' expectations—of beauty, quality, and value.

Designed by Heather Zschock
Cover illustration © Jennifer Orkin Lewis | Jennifer Nelson Artists, Inc.

Copyright © 2019
Peter Pauper Press, Inc.
202 Mamaroneck Avenue
White Plains, NY 10601 USA
All rights reserved
ISBN 978-1-4413-3293-6
Printed in China
7 6 5 4 3 2 1

Visit us at www.peterpauper.com

*Wear gratitude like a cloak and it will feed
every corner of your life.*

Rumi

Conscious acknowledgment of what is good in our lives renders us, each day, more open to welcome the joys and weather the hardships that come our way. In these daily pages, take stock of the things that move you to gratitude, and appreciate them more fully.

Here are some gratitude hints for the journey:

- If something makes you feel happy, savor the moment and appreciate it deeply.

- Notice the little gifts each day brings—the first firefly of the season, an unexpected compliment, the glow of a sunset.

- When something wonderful happens, write about it later in detail, so you can revisit it vividly.

- Look for simple ways to help others. When you can, improve someone's day with a random act of kindness.

- When someone goes out of their way for you, express your appreciation.

In the daily practice of gratitude, we discover what we value. Noticing—and appreciating—the gifts of each day cultivates a grateful heart. In every facet of our lives, gratitude is a path to a richer and more joyful existence.

MY GRATITUDE LIST

How I can practice daily gratitude.
What people and things make your life better on a daily basis, and how can you acknowledge them?

Ways I can pay it forward.
How can you practice kindness and generosity toward others?

What I am grateful for today: _____ Date: _____

_____

_____

_____

_____

_____

_____

_____

What I am grateful for today: _____ Date: _____

_____

_____

_____

_____

_____

_____

_____

What I am grateful for today: _____ Date: _____

_____

_____

_____

_____

_____

_____

What I am grateful for today: _____ Date: _____

_____

_____

_____

_____

_____

_____

_____

What I am grateful for today: _____ Date: _____

_____

_____

_____

_____

_____

_____

_____

Acts of kindness toward others this week: _____

What I am grateful for today: _____ Date: _____

_____

_____

_____

_____

_____

_____

_____

What I am grateful for today: _____ Date: _____

_____

_____

_____

_____

_____

_____

_____

What I am grateful for today: _____ Date: _____

_____

_____

_____

_____

_____

_____

_____

What I am grateful for today: _____ Date: _____

_____

_____

_____

_____

_____

_____

_____

What I am grateful for today: _____ Date: _____

_____

_____

_____

_____

_____

_____

_____

Acts of kindness toward others this week: _____

_____

_____

_____

_____

_____

_____

_____

What I am grateful for today: _____ Date: _____

_____

_____

_____

_____

_____

_____

What I am grateful for today: _____ Date: _____

_____

_____

_____

_____

_____

_____

What I am grateful for today: _____ Date: _____

_____

_____

_____

_____

_____

_____

What I am grateful for today: Date:

_____

_____

_____

_____

_____

_____

What I am grateful for today: Date:

_____

_____

_____

_____

_____

_____

Acts of kindness toward others this week:

_____

_____

_____

_____

_____

_____

_____

What I am grateful for today: _____ Date: _____

_____

_____

_____

_____

_____

_____

_____

What I am grateful for today: _____ Date: _____

_____

_____

_____

_____

_____

_____

_____

What I am grateful for today: _____ Date: _____

_____

_____

_____

_____

_____

_____

_____

What I am grateful for today: _____ Date: _____

_____

_____

_____

_____

_____

_____

_____

What I am grateful for today: _____ Date: _____

_____

_____

_____

_____

_____

_____

_____

Acts of kindness toward others this week: _____

What I am grateful for today: _____ Date: _____

_____

_____

_____

_____

_____

_____

_____

What I am grateful for today: _____ Date: _____

_____

_____

_____

_____

_____

_____

_____

What I am grateful for today: _____ Date: _____

_____

_____

_____

_____

_____

_____

_____

What I am grateful for today: _____ Date: _____

_____

_____

_____

_____

_____

_____

_____

What I am grateful for today: _____ Date: _____

_____

_____

_____

_____

_____

_____

_____

Acts of kindness toward others this week: _____

What I am grateful for today: _____ Date: _____

What I am grateful for today: _____ Date: _____

What I am grateful for today: _____ Date: _____

What I am grateful for today: Date:

What I am grateful for today: Date:

Acts of kindness toward others this week:

I would maintain that
thanks are the highest
form of thought;
and that gratitude is
happiness doubled
by wonder.

G. K. Chesterton

Who are the people in my life I am most grateful for:

What I am grateful for today: Date:

_____

_____

_____

_____

_____

_____

_____

_____

What I am grateful for today: Date:

_____

_____

_____

_____

_____

_____

_____

_____

What I am grateful for today: Date:

_____

_____

_____

_____

_____

_____

_____

_____

What I am grateful for today: _____ Date: _____

_____

_____

_____

_____

_____

_____

_____

What I am grateful for today: _____ Date: _____

_____

_____

_____

_____

_____

_____

_____

Acts of kindness toward others this week: _____

What I am grateful for today: _____ Date: _____

_____

_____

_____

_____

_____

_____

What I am grateful for today: _____ Date: _____

_____

_____

_____

_____

_____

_____

What I am grateful for today: _____ Date: _____

_____

_____

_____

_____

_____

_____

What I am grateful for today: _____ Date: _____

_____
_____
_____
_____
_____
_____
_____

What I am grateful for today: _____ Date: _____

_____
_____
_____
_____
_____
_____

Acts of kindness toward others this week: _____

What I am grateful for today: _____ Date: _____

_____

_____

_____

_____

_____

_____

_____

What I am grateful for today: _____ Date: _____

_____

_____

_____

_____

_____

_____

_____

What I am grateful for today: _____ Date: _____

_____

_____

_____

_____

_____

_____

_____

What I am grateful for today: _____ Date: _____

_____

_____

_____

_____

_____

_____

_____

What I am grateful for today: _____ Date: _____

_____

_____

_____

_____

_____

_____

_____

Acts of kindness toward others this week: _____

_____

_____

_____

_____

_____

_____

_____

What I am grateful for today: Date:

_____

_____

_____

_____

_____

_____

_____

What I am grateful for today: Date:

_____

_____

_____

_____

_____

_____

_____

What I am grateful for today: Date:

_____

_____

_____

_____

_____

_____

_____

What I am grateful for today: _____ Date: _____

_____

_____

_____

_____

_____

_____

_____

What I am grateful for today: _____ Date: _____

_____

_____

_____

_____

_____

_____

_____

Acts of kindness toward others this week: _____

_____

_____

_____

_____

_____

_____

What I am grateful for today: _____ Date: _____

What I am grateful for today: _____ Date: _____

What I am grateful for today: _____ Date: _____

What I am grateful for today: _____ Date: _____

_____

_____

_____

_____

_____

_____

_____

What I am grateful for today: _____ Date: _____

_____

_____

_____

_____

_____

_____

_____

Acts of kindness toward others this week: _____

_____

_____

_____

_____

_____

_____

_____

What I am grateful for today: _____ Date: _____

_____
_____
_____
_____
_____
_____
_____

What I am grateful for today: _____ Date: _____

_____
_____
_____
_____
_____
_____
_____

What I am grateful for today: _____ Date: _____

_____
_____
_____
_____
_____
_____
_____

What I am grateful for today: Date:

What I am grateful for today: Date:

Acts of kindness toward others this week:

If the only prayer
you say in your life is
"thank you,"
that would suffice.

Meister Eckhart

Things I'm grateful for that I sometimes take for granted:

What I am grateful for today: _____ Date: _____

What I am grateful for today: _____ Date: _____

What I am grateful for today: _____ Date: _____

What I am grateful for today: Date:

_____

_____

_____

_____

_____

_____

_____

What I am grateful for today: Date:

_____

_____

_____

_____

_____

_____

_____

Acts of kindness toward others this week:

_____

_____

_____

_____

_____

_____

_____

What I am grateful for today: Date:

_____

_____

_____

_____

_____

_____

_____

What I am grateful for today: Date:

_____

_____

_____

_____

_____

_____

_____

What I am grateful for today: Date:

_____

_____

_____

_____

_____

_____

_____

What I am grateful for today: _____ Date: _____

_____

_____

_____

_____

_____

_____

_____

What I am grateful for today: _____ Date: _____

_____

_____

_____

_____

_____

_____

_____

Acts of kindness toward others this week: _____

_____

_____

_____

_____

_____

_____

_____

What I am grateful for today: _____ Date: _____

_____
_____
_____
_____
_____
_____
_____

What I am grateful for today: _____ Date: _____

_____
_____
_____
_____
_____
_____
_____

What I am grateful for today: _____ Date: _____

_____
_____
_____
_____
_____
_____
_____

What I am grateful for today: Date:

_____

_____

_____

_____

_____

_____

What I am grateful for today: Date:

_____

_____

_____

_____

_____

_____

Acts of kindness toward others this week:

_____

_____

_____

_____

_____

What I am grateful for today: Date:

_____
_____
_____
_____
_____
_____
_____

What I am grateful for today: Date:

_____
_____
_____
_____
_____
_____
_____

What I am grateful for today: Date:

_____
_____
_____
_____
_____
_____
_____

What I am grateful for today: _____ Date: _____

_____

_____

_____

_____

_____

_____

_____

What I am grateful for today: _____ Date: _____

_____

_____

_____

_____

_____

_____

_____

Acts of kindness toward others this week: _____

_____

_____

_____

_____

_____

_____

_____

What I am grateful for today: Date:

_____

_____

_____

_____

_____

_____

What I am grateful for today: Date:

_____

_____

_____

_____

_____

_____

What I am grateful for today: Date:

_____

_____

_____

_____

_____

_____

What I am grateful for today: _____ Date: _____

_____

_____

_____

_____

_____

_____

_____

What I am grateful for today: _____ Date: _____

_____

_____

_____

_____

_____

_____

_____

Acts of kindness toward others this week: _____

_____

_____

_____

_____

_____

_____

_____

What I am grateful for today: Date:

What I am grateful for today: Date:

What I am grateful for today: Date:

What I am grateful for today: Date:

_____

_____

_____

_____

_____

_____

_____

What I am grateful for today: Date:

_____

_____

_____

_____

_____

_____

Acts of kindness toward others this week:

There are flowers everywhere for those who want to see them.

Henri Matisse

How might I expand my concept of gratitude:

What I am grateful for today: _____ Date: _____

_____
_____
_____
_____
_____
_____
_____

What I am grateful for today: _____ Date: _____

_____
_____
_____
_____
_____
_____
_____

What I am grateful for today: _____ Date: _____

_____
_____
_____
_____
_____
_____
_____

What I am grateful for today: _____ Date: _____

What I am grateful for today: _____ Date: _____

Acts of kindness toward others this week: _____

What I am grateful for today: _____ Date: _____

_____

_____

_____

_____

_____

_____

What I am grateful for today: _____ Date: _____

_____

_____

_____

_____

_____

_____

What I am grateful for today: _____ Date: _____

_____

_____

_____

_____

_____

_____

What I am grateful for today: _____ Date: _____

_____
_____
_____
_____
_____
_____
_____

What I am grateful for today: _____ Date: _____

_____
_____
_____
_____
_____
_____
_____

Acts of kindness toward others this week: _____

_____
_____
_____
_____
_____
_____
_____

What I am grateful for today: _____ Date: _____

_____

_____

_____

_____

_____

_____

_____

What I am grateful for today: _____ Date: _____

_____

_____

_____

_____

_____

_____

_____

What I am grateful for today: _____ Date: _____

_____

_____

_____

_____

_____

_____

_____

What I am grateful for today: _____ Date: _____

_____

_____

_____

_____

_____

_____

_____

What I am grateful for today: _____ Date: _____

_____

_____

_____

_____

_____

_____

_____

Acts of kindness toward others this week: _____

_____

_____

_____

_____

_____

_____

What I am grateful for today: _____ Date: _____

_____

_____

_____

_____

_____

_____

What I am grateful for today: _____ Date: _____

_____

_____

_____

_____

_____

_____

What I am grateful for today: _____ Date: _____

_____

_____

_____

_____

_____

_____

What I am grateful for today: _____ Date: _____

_____

_____

_____

_____

_____

_____

_____

What I am grateful for today: _____ Date: _____

_____

_____

_____

_____

_____

_____

Acts of kindness toward others this week: _____

_____

_____

_____

_____

_____

_____

What I am grateful for today: Date:

What I am grateful for today: Date:

What I am grateful for today: Date:

What I am grateful for today: _____ Date: _____

_____

_____

_____

_____

_____

_____

_____

What I am grateful for today: _____ Date: _____

_____

_____

_____

_____

_____

_____

_____

Acts of kindness toward others this week: _____

_____

_____

_____

_____

_____

_____

_____

What I am grateful for today: Date:

What I am grateful for today: Date:

What I am grateful for today: Date:

What I am grateful for today: _____ Date: _____

_____

_____

_____

_____

_____

_____

_____

What I am grateful for today: _____ Date: _____

_____

_____

_____

_____

_____

_____

_____

Acts of kindness toward others this week: _____

The true purpose
of a present is to
be received.

Marie Kondo

What are some gifts I can share:

What I am grateful for today: _____ Date: _____

_____

_____

_____

_____

_____

_____

_____

What I am grateful for today: _____ Date: _____

_____

_____

_____

_____

_____

_____

_____

What I am grateful for today: _____ Date: _____

_____

_____

_____

_____

_____

_____

_____

What I am grateful for today: _____ Date: _____

_____

_____

_____

_____

_____

_____

What I am grateful for today: _____ Date: _____

_____

_____

_____

_____

_____

_____

Acts of kindness toward others this week: _____

_____

_____

_____

_____

_____

_____

_____

What I am grateful for today: _____ Date: _____

_____

_____

_____

_____

_____

_____

What I am grateful for today: _____ Date: _____

_____

_____

_____

_____

_____

_____

What I am grateful for today: _____ Date: _____

_____

_____

_____

_____

_____

_____

What I am grateful for today: Date:

What I am grateful for today: Date:

Acts of kindness toward others this week:

What I am grateful for today: _____ Date: _____

_____
_____
_____
_____
_____
_____
_____

What I am grateful for today: _____ Date: _____

_____
_____
_____
_____
_____
_____
_____

What I am grateful for today: _____ Date: _____

_____
_____
_____
_____
_____
_____
_____

What I am grateful for today: _____ Date: _____

_____

_____

_____

_____

_____

_____

_____

What I am grateful for today: _____ Date: _____

_____

_____

_____

_____

_____

_____

_____

Acts of kindness toward others this week: _____

What I am grateful for today: Date:

_____

_____

_____

_____

_____

_____

_____

What I am grateful for today: Date:

_____

_____

_____

_____

_____

_____

_____

What I am grateful for today: Date:

_____

_____

_____

_____

_____

_____

_____

What I am grateful for today: _____ Date: _____

_____

_____

_____

_____

_____

_____

_____

What I am grateful for today: _____ Date: _____

_____

_____

_____

_____

_____

_____

_____

Acts of kindness toward others this week: _____

What I am grateful for today: Date:

_____

_____

_____

_____

_____

_____

What I am grateful for today: Date:

_____

_____

_____

_____

_____

_____

What I am grateful for today: Date:

_____

_____

_____

_____

_____

_____

What I am grateful for today: _____ Date: _____

_____

_____

_____

_____

_____

_____

_____

What I am grateful for today: _____ Date: _____

_____

_____

_____

_____

_____

_____

_____

Acts of kindness toward others this week: _____

What I am grateful for today: Date:

_____

_____

_____

_____

_____

_____

_____

What I am grateful for today: Date:

_____

_____

_____

_____

_____

_____

_____

What I am grateful for today: Date:

_____

_____

_____

_____

_____

_____

_____

What I am grateful for today: _____ Date: _____

_____

_____

_____

_____

_____

_____

_____

What I am grateful for today: _____ Date: _____

_____

_____

_____

_____

_____

_____

_____

Acts of kindness toward others this week: _____

Happiness is
itself a kind of
gratitude.

Joseph Wood Krutch

When gratitude lightens up my life:

What I am grateful for today: _____ Date: _____

_____

_____

_____

_____

_____

_____

What I am grateful for today: _____ Date: _____

_____

_____

_____

_____

_____

_____

What I am grateful for today: _____ Date: _____

_____

_____

_____

_____

_____

_____

What I am grateful for today: _____ Date: _____

_____

_____

_____

_____

_____

_____

_____

What I am grateful for today: _____ Date: _____

_____

_____

_____

_____

_____

_____

_____

Acts of kindness toward others this week: _____

What I am grateful for today: _____ Date: _____

_____

_____

_____

_____

_____

_____

_____

What I am grateful for today: _____ Date: _____

_____

_____

_____

_____

_____

_____

_____

What I am grateful for today: _____ Date: _____

_____

_____

_____

_____

_____

_____

_____

What I am grateful for today: _____ Date: _____

_____

_____

_____

_____

_____

_____

What I am grateful for today: _____ Date: _____

_____

_____

_____

_____

_____

_____

Acts of kindness toward others this week: _____

_____

_____

_____

_____

_____

_____

_____

What I am grateful for today: _____ Date: _____

_____

_____

_____

_____

_____

_____

_____

What I am grateful for today: _____ Date: _____

_____

_____

_____

_____

_____

_____

_____

What I am grateful for today: _____ Date: _____

_____

_____

_____

_____

_____

_____

_____

What I am grateful for today: Date:

What I am grateful for today: Date:

Acts of kindness toward others this week:

What I am grateful for today: _____ Date: _____

_____

_____

_____

_____

_____

_____

What I am grateful for today: _____ Date: _____

_____

_____

_____

_____

_____

_____

What I am grateful for today: _____ Date: _____

_____

_____

_____

_____

_____

_____

What I am grateful for today: _____ Date: _____

_____

_____

_____

_____

_____

_____

What I am grateful for today: _____ Date: _____

_____

_____

_____

_____

_____

_____

Acts of kindness toward others this week: _____

What I am grateful for today: Date:

What I am grateful for today: Date:

What I am grateful for today: Date:

What I am grateful for today: _____ Date: _____

_____

_____

_____

_____

_____

_____

What I am grateful for today: _____ Date: _____

_____

_____

_____

_____

_____

_____

Acts of kindness toward others this week: _____

_____

_____

_____

_____

_____

_____

_____

What I am grateful for today: _____ Date: _____

_____
_____
_____
_____
_____
_____
_____

What I am grateful for today: _____ Date: _____

_____
_____
_____
_____
_____
_____
_____

What I am grateful for today: _____ Date: _____

_____
_____
_____
_____
_____
_____
_____

What I am grateful for today: _____ Date: _____

_____

_____

_____

_____

_____

_____

What I am grateful for today: _____ Date: _____

_____

_____

_____

_____

_____

_____

Acts of kindness toward others this week: _____

_____

_____

_____

_____

_____

_____

*The present moment is
filled with joy and happiness.
If you are attentive,
you will see it.*

Thich Nhat Hanh

Ways I can be more attentive in my daily life:

What I am grateful for today: _____ Date: _____

_____

_____

_____

_____

_____

_____

_____

What I am grateful for today: _____ Date: _____

_____

_____

_____

_____

_____

_____

_____

What I am grateful for today: _____ Date: _____

_____

_____

_____

_____

_____

_____

_____

What I am grateful for today: _____ Date: _____

_____

_____

_____

_____

_____

_____

_____

What I am grateful for today: _____ Date: _____

_____

_____

_____

_____

_____

_____

_____

Acts of kindness toward others this week: _____

What I am grateful for today: _____ Date: _____

_____

_____

_____

_____

_____

_____

What I am grateful for today: _____ Date: _____

_____

_____

_____

_____

_____

_____

What I am grateful for today: _____ Date: _____

_____

_____

_____

_____

_____

_____

What I am grateful for today: Date:

What I am grateful for today: Date:

Acts of kindness toward others this week:

What I am grateful for today: Date:

_____

_____

_____

_____

_____

_____

_____

What I am grateful for today: Date:

_____

_____

_____

_____

_____

_____

_____

What I am grateful for today: Date:

_____

_____

_____

_____

_____

_____

_____

What I am grateful for today: _____ Date: _____

_____

_____

_____

_____

_____

_____

_____

What I am grateful for today: _____ Date: _____

_____

_____

_____

_____

_____

_____

_____

Acts of kindness toward others this week: _____

_____

_____

_____

_____

_____

_____

_____

What I am grateful for today: _____ Date: _____

_____
_____
_____
_____
_____
_____
_____
_____

What I am grateful for today: _____ Date: _____

_____
_____
_____
_____
_____
_____
_____
_____

What I am grateful for today: _____ Date: _____

_____
_____
_____
_____
_____
_____
_____
_____

What I am grateful for today: Date:

What I am grateful for today: Date:

Acts of kindness toward others this week:

What I am grateful for today: _____ Date: _____

_____

_____

_____

_____

_____

_____

_____

What I am grateful for today: _____ Date: _____

_____

_____

_____

_____

_____

_____

_____

What I am grateful for today: _____ Date: _____

_____

_____

_____

_____

_____

_____

_____

<u>What I am grateful for today:</u>   Date:

<u>What I am grateful for today:</u>   Date:

<u>Acts of kindness toward others this week:</u>

What I am grateful for today: Date:

What I am grateful for today: Date:

What I am grateful for today: Date:

What I am grateful for today: _____ Date: _____

_____

_____

_____

_____

_____

_____

_____

What I am grateful for today: _____ Date: _____

_____

_____

_____

_____

_____

_____

_____

Acts of kindness toward others this week: _____

_____

_____

_____

_____

_____

_____

_____

In the end, maybe it's wiser to surrender before the miraculous scope of human generosity and to just keep saying thank you, forever and sincerely, for as long as we have voices.

Elizabeth Gilbert

Acts of kindness I am thankful for:

What I am grateful for today: _____ Date: _____

_____

_____

_____

_____

_____

_____

What I am grateful for today: _____ Date: _____

_____

_____

_____

_____

_____

_____

What I am grateful for today: _____ Date: _____

_____

_____

_____

_____

_____

_____

What I am grateful for today: Date:

_____

_____

_____

_____

_____

_____

_____

What I am grateful for today: Date:

_____

_____

_____

_____

_____

_____

_____

Acts of kindness toward others this week:

What I am grateful for today: Date:

_____

_____

_____

_____

_____

_____

What I am grateful for today: Date:

_____

_____

_____

_____

_____

_____

What I am grateful for today: Date:

_____

_____

_____

_____

_____

_____

What I am grateful for today: Date:

What I am grateful for today: Date:

Acts of kindness toward others this week:

What I am grateful for today: _____ Date: _____

_____

_____

_____

_____

_____

_____

_____

What I am grateful for today: _____ Date: _____

_____

_____

_____

_____

_____

_____

_____

What I am grateful for today: _____ Date: _____

_____

_____

_____

_____

_____

_____

_____

What I am grateful for today: _____ Date: _____

_____

_____

_____

_____

_____

_____

_____

What I am grateful for today: _____ Date: _____

_____

_____

_____

_____

_____

_____

_____

Acts of kindness toward others this week: _____

What I am grateful for today: _____ Date: _____

_____

_____

_____

_____

_____

_____

What I am grateful for today: _____ Date: _____

_____

_____

_____

_____

_____

_____

What I am grateful for today: _____ Date: _____

_____

_____

_____

_____

_____

_____

What I am grateful for today: _____ Date: _____

_____

_____

_____

_____

_____

_____

_____

What I am grateful for today: _____ Date: _____

_____

_____

_____

_____

_____

_____

Acts of kindness toward others this week: _____

_____

_____

_____

_____

_____

_____

What I am grateful for today: Date:

What I am grateful for today: Date:

What I am grateful for today: Date:

What I am grateful for today: _____ Date: _____

_____

_____

_____

_____

_____

_____

What I am grateful for today: _____ Date: _____

_____

_____

_____

_____

_____

_____

Acts of kindness toward others this week: _____

_____

_____

_____

_____

_____

_____

What I am grateful for today: _____ Date: _____

_____

_____

_____

_____

_____

_____

_____

What I am grateful for today: _____ Date: _____

_____

_____

_____

_____

_____

_____

_____

What I am grateful for today: _____ Date: _____

_____

_____

_____

_____

_____

_____

_____

What I am grateful for today: _____ Date: _____

_____

_____

_____

_____

_____

_____

What I am grateful for today: _____ Date: _____

_____

_____

_____

_____

_____

_____

Acts of kindness toward others this week: _____

_____

_____

_____

_____

_____

_____

What separates privilege from entitlement is gratitude.

Brené Brown

Ways I am privileged, and how I can give back:

_____

_____

_____

_____

_____

_____

_____

_____

_____

_____

_____

_____

_____

_____

_____

_____

_____

_____

_____

_____

What I am grateful for today: Date:

What I am grateful for today: Date:

What I am grateful for today: Date:

What I am grateful for today: Date:

_____

_____

_____

_____

_____

_____

_____

What I am grateful for today: Date:

_____

_____

_____

_____

_____

_____

_____

Acts of kindness toward others this week:

_____

_____

_____

_____

_____

_____

_____

_____

What I am grateful for today: _____ Date: _____

_____

_____

_____

_____

_____

_____

_____

What I am grateful for today: _____ Date: _____

_____

_____

_____

_____

_____

_____

_____

What I am grateful for today: _____ Date: _____

_____

_____

_____

_____

_____

_____

_____

What I am grateful for today: _____ Date: _____

_____

_____

_____

_____

_____

_____

What I am grateful for today: _____ Date: _____

_____

_____

_____

_____

_____

_____

Acts of kindness toward others this week: _____

_____

_____

_____

_____

_____

_____

What I am grateful for today: Date:

_____

_____

_____

_____

_____

_____

_____

What I am grateful for today: Date:

_____

_____

_____

_____

_____

_____

_____

What I am grateful for today: Date:

_____

_____

_____

_____

_____

_____

_____

What I am grateful for today: _____ Date: _____

_____

_____

_____

_____

_____

_____

_____

What I am grateful for today: _____ Date: _____

_____

_____

_____

_____

_____

_____

_____

Acts of kindness toward others this week: _____

_____

_____

_____

_____

_____

_____

_____

What I am grateful for today: _____ Date: _____

_____

_____

_____

_____

_____

_____

_____

What I am grateful for today: _____ Date: _____

_____

_____

_____

_____

_____

_____

_____

What I am grateful for today: _____ Date: _____

_____

_____

_____

_____

_____

_____

_____

What I am grateful for today: _____ Date: _____

_____

_____

_____

_____

_____

_____

What I am grateful for today: _____ Date: _____

_____

_____

_____

_____

_____

_____

Acts of kindness toward others this week: _____

What I am grateful for today: _____ Date: _____

_____

_____

_____

_____

_____

_____

_____

What I am grateful for today: _____ Date: _____

_____

_____

_____

_____

_____

_____

_____

What I am grateful for today: _____ Date: _____

_____

_____

_____

_____

_____

_____

_____

What I am grateful for today: _____ Date: _____

What I am grateful for today: _____ Date: _____

Acts of kindness toward others this week:

What I am grateful for today: _____ Date: _____

_____

_____

_____

_____

_____

_____

What I am grateful for today: _____ Date: _____

_____

_____

_____

_____

_____

_____

What I am grateful for today: _____ Date: _____

_____

_____

_____

_____

_____

_____

What I am grateful for today: Date:

_____

_____

_____

_____

_____

_____

_____

What I am grateful for today: Date:

_____

_____

_____

_____

_____

_____

_____

Acts of kindness toward others this week:

For each new morning
with its light,
For rest and shelter
of the night,
For health and food,
for love and friends,
For everything Thy
goodness sends.

Ralph Waldo Emerson

Everyday things I am grateful for:

What I am grateful for today: Date:

What I am grateful for today: Date:

What I am grateful for today: Date:

What I am grateful for today: _____ Date: _____

_____

_____

_____

_____

_____

_____

_____

What I am grateful for today: _____ Date: _____

_____

_____

_____

_____

_____

_____

_____

Acts of kindness toward others this week: _____

_____

_____

_____

_____

_____

_____

_____

What I am grateful for today: _____ Date: _____

_____

_____

_____

_____

_____

_____

_____

What I am grateful for today: _____ Date: _____

_____

_____

_____

_____

_____

_____

_____

What I am grateful for today: _____ Date: _____

_____

_____

_____

_____

_____

_____

_____

What I am grateful for today: Date:

What I am grateful for today: Date:

Acts of kindness toward others this week:

What I am grateful for today: Date:

_____

_____

_____

_____

_____

_____

_____

What I am grateful for today: Date:

_____

_____

_____

_____

_____

_____

_____

What I am grateful for today: Date:

_____

_____

_____

_____

_____

_____

_____

What I am grateful for today: _____ Date: _____

_____

_____

_____

_____

_____

_____

_____

What I am grateful for today: _____ Date: _____

_____

_____

_____

_____

_____

_____

Acts of kindness toward others this week:

_____

_____

_____

_____

_____

_____

_____

What I am grateful for today: _____ Date: _____

_____

_____

_____

_____

_____

_____

_____

_____

What I am grateful for today: _____ Date: _____

_____

_____

_____

_____

_____

_____

_____

_____

What I am grateful for today: _____ Date: _____

_____

_____

_____

_____

_____

_____

_____

_____

What I am grateful for today: _____ Date: _____

_____

_____

_____

_____

_____

_____

What I am grateful for today: _____ Date: _____

_____

_____

_____

_____

_____

_____

Acts of kindness toward others this week: _____

_____

_____

_____

_____

_____

_____

What I am grateful for today: _____ Date: _____

_____

_____

_____

_____

_____

_____

What I am grateful for today: _____ Date: _____

_____

_____

_____

_____

_____

_____

What I am grateful for today: _____ Date: _____

_____

_____

_____

_____

_____

_____

What I am grateful for today: Date:

_____

_____

_____

_____

_____

_____

_____

What I am grateful for today: Date:

_____

_____

_____

_____

_____

_____

_____

Acts of kindness toward others this week:

_____

_____

_____

_____

_____

_____

_____

What I am grateful for today: _____ Date: _____

_____

_____

_____

_____

_____

_____

_____

What I am grateful for today: _____ Date: _____

_____

_____

_____

_____

_____

_____

_____

What I am grateful for today: _____ Date: _____

_____

_____

_____

_____

_____

_____

_____

What I am grateful for today: _____ Date: _____

_____

_____

_____

_____

_____

_____

_____

What I am grateful for today: _____ Date: _____

_____

_____

_____

_____

_____

_____

_____

Acts of kindness toward others this week: _____

_____

_____

_____

_____

_____

_____

_____

Can you see the holiness
in those things you take
for granted—a paved road
or a washing machine?
If you concentrate on finding
what is good in every situation,
you will discover that your life
will suddenly be filled
with gratitude, a feeling that
nurtures the soul.

Rabbi Harold Kushner

Made in the USA
Las Vegas, NV
26 February 2024

86353599R00085